Who Lives in a Barn?

GOATS

KERRI MAZZARELLA

Table of Contents

A Starfish Book

SEAHORSE PUBLISHING

Teaching Tips for Caregivers:

As a caregiver, you can help your child succeed in school by giving them a strong foundation in language and literacy skills and a desire to learn to read.

This book helps children grow by letting them practice reading skills.

Reading for pleasure and interest will help your child to develop reading skills and will give your child the opportunity to practice these skills in meaningful ways.

- Encourage your child to read on her own at home
- Encourage your child to practice reading aloud
- Encourage activities that require reading
- Establish a reading time
- Talk with your child
- Give your child writing materials

Teaching Tips for Teachers:

Research shows that one of the best ways for students to learn a new topic is to read about it.

Before Reading

- Read the "Words to Know" and discuss the meaning of each word.
- Read the back cover to see what the book is about.

During Reading

- When a student gets to a word that is unknown, ask them to look at the rest of the sentence to find clues to help with the meaning of the unknown word.
- Ask the student to write down any pages of the book that were confusing to them.

After Reading

- Discuss the main idea of the book.
- Ask students to give one detail that they learned in the book by showing a text dependent answer from the book.

Goats

You can find a **barn** on a farm.

Animals live in a barn.

One animal is the goat.

Goat **breeds** have different colors and sizes.

Goats can weigh 44 to 310 pounds (20 to 140 kilograms).

They can be black, brown, white, or gray.

Some have spots!

A male goat is called a billy.

A female goat is called a nanny.

Baby goats are called kids.

Both male and female goats can have a beard!

A nanny can give birth to six kids at one time.

Kids can stand just a few minutes after being born.

Kids have a close bond with each other and their mom.

Nannies feed kids milk to help them grow strong.

Goats are social animals.

They do not like to be alone.

They live in a group called a **herd**.

A goat away from its herd will be scared and upset.

Goats communicate with each other in different ways.

They make sounds called bleats.

They move their ears, tails, and faces.

Myotonic goats are also known as "fainting goats." They fall over onto the ground when they are startled or excited.

Goats are **herbivores**.

They like to eat grass, hay, and shrubs.

Goats love to climb on things. They can jump up to five feet (two meters).

Goats are useful to people.

They provide meat to eat.

They give milk to drink.

Butter, cheese, and yogurt can all be made from goat milk.

Goats also provide fur.

It is used to make **fabric** all over the world.

Cashmere is a soft, expensive wool that is made from the fur of certain goats. It takes two goats to make just one cashmere sweater!

Goats live all over the world.

They can **adapt** to almost any environment.

China has more goats than any other country.

Words to Know

adapt (uh-DAPT): to change to fit in with the surroundings

barn (bahrn): a large farm building where crops, animals, and equipment are kept

breeds (breedz): types of animals; for example, poodle is one dog breed

fabric (FAB-rik): cloth or material for making clothes and other items

herbivores (HUR-buh-vorz): animals that eat only plants

herd (hurd): a large number of animals that stay together or move together

Index

Comprehension Questions

1. A baby goat is called
   a. a calf.
   b. a chick.
   c. a kid.
2. **True or False:** A male goat is called a nanny.
3. What is made from goat milk?
   a. meat
   b. cheese
   c. salad
4. **True or False:** Goats are herbivores.
5. Goats talk to each other with sounds called
   a. bleats. **b.** moos. **c.** clucks.

Answers
1. c 2. False 3. b 4. True 5. a

About the Author

Kerri Mazzarella lives in Florida and enjoys reading and writing. She loves animals. Kerri likes to visit the farm with her children. Her favorite barn animal is the horse.

Written by: Kerri Mazzarella
Design by: Kathy Walsh
Editor: Kim Thompson

Photographs/Shutterstock: Cover & TOC White Space Illustrations, Vectorfair, PixHom, Manfred Ruckszio; p 4-23 aPhoenix photographer; p 3 Anton Havelaar; p 5 Elina Litovkina; p 6 Joseph Scott Photography; p 7 imagevixen; p 8 CreativeFireStock; p 9 Wichai Prasomsri1; p 10 Moisieiev Igor; p 11 Aggie 11; p 13 Tanya May; p 14 flysnowfly; p 15 Alla Laurent; p 16 Irina Rostokina; p 17 Jenoche; p 18 LTRG; p 19 Alessandro Cristiano; p 20, 21 Daniel Andis

Library of Congress PCN Data
Goats / Kerri Mazzarella
Who Lives in a Barn?
ISBN 978-1-6389-7964-7 (hard cover)
ISBN 979-8-8873-5023-3 (paperback)
ISBN 979-8-8873-5082-0 (EPUB)
ISBN 979-8-8873-5141-4 (eBook)
Library of Congress Control Number: 2022941900

Printed in the United States of America.

Seahorse Publishing Company
www.seahorsepub.com

Published in the United States
Seahorse Publishing
PO Box 771325
Coral Springs, FL 33077

SEAHORSE PUBLISHING